PENGUIN BOOKS
LAUGH WITH LAXMAN: VOLUME II

Rasipuram Krishnaswamy Laxman was born in Mysore in 1924. He began cartooning for the *Free Press Journal,* a newspaper in Bombay, in 1947, soon after he graduated from the University of Mysore. Six months later he joined the *Times of India* as staff cartoonist; he continues to draw for the newspaper even today.

R.K. Laxman has written and published numerous short stories, essays and travel articles, some of which have been collected in the book, *The Distorted Mirror.* He has also written three works of fiction, *The Hotel Riviera, The Messenger* and *Servants of India*, all of which have been published by Penguin Books. Penguin has also published several collections of Laxman's cartoons in the series The Best of Laxman and Laugh with Laxman. *The Tunnel of Time*, Laxman's autobiography, is also available from Penguin.

R.K. Laxman has won numerous awards for his cartoons, including Asia's top journalism award, the Ramon Magsaysay Award, in 1984. The University of Marathwada and the University of Delhi have conferred honorary Doctor of Literature degrees on him. In 2005, the Government of India honoured him with the Padma Vibhushan.

R.K. Laxman lives in Mumbai.

R.K. Laxman

LAUGH WITH LAXMAN

Volume II

PENGUIN BOOKS

An imprint of Penguin Random House

PENGUIN BOOKS

USA | Canada | UK | Ireland | Australia
New Zealand | India | South Africa | China | Singapore

Penguin Books is part of the Penguin Random House group of companies
whose addresses can be found at global.penguinrandomhouse.com

Published by Penguin Random House India Pvt. Ltd
4th Floor, Capital Tower 1, MG Road,
Gurugram 122 002, Haryana, India

Penguin
Random House
India

First published by Penguin Books India 2002

Copyright © R.K. Laxman 2002

All rights reserved

10 9 8 7 6 5

ISBN 9780143028680

Typeset in Sabon by S.R. Enterprises, New Delhi

Printed at Manipal Technologies Limited, India

www.penguin.co.in

I know you have taken great care. I hope you have switched off the main switch!

You are going to be transferred next week.

High-level inquiry? Please, Sir, appoint a low-level inquiry to look into my irregularities in view of my seniority!

Transfer that man here; there is an allegation of corruption against him. Transfer this officer to that post—there is a charge against him too!

Oh, don't disturb him, Sir. You don't want to have a strike on your hands, do you?

Please have it. We have cut down on expenditure on business lunches as an economy measure, you see.

The Chief is not a vindictive type, I agree. But I don't like his idea of punishment for mistakes committed!

That happened when our computers were infected with a virus and went out of commission.

That high powered Sales Executive we hired not only sold the entire stock but the whole factory as well, Sir!

One nice thing about this wild life sanctuary is that all the animals are tourist friendly!

Oh my! We have to shoot the entire epic all over again!
We forgot to ask him to remove his glasses!

I have almost discovered it, Professor—a soft drink! It's 90% soft!

...*and the resolution as passed reads, '...it is resolved that retirement age will be raised from 85 to 90...!'*

No wonder it is not taking off. Those fools are counting up instead of counting down!

It is still not selling! We must try offering a washing machine free along with it!

Looks formidable all right! But has he considered its practical applicability in a crisis?

'What do you mean, "Dr Livingstone, I presume?" Oh no,
I used to be Tarzan!'

17

There was nothing wrong, Sir. It wouldn't start because the petrol tank was empty! Here is the bill for Rs 2,471 for finding it out.

This is an all-purpose ad, Sir. It can be used for washing machines, lipsticks, ice-cream, cars, skin care products, etc. etc....

I told you to take the other road. The speed breaker is deadly in this!

I take any route to go to the office that doesn't have traffic jams.

*That would be just enough, Your Honour, by way of
laying the foundation stone.*

Forget your private quarrels and start fighting, please!
People are waiting.

*Conditions are excellent here, young man—he was
brought here for experimental purposes and today he
heads the department!*

What a marvellous thing—it must be Japanese—the tiniest colour TV in the world!

It's a second-hand carpet. I bought it from an oil sheikh.

We are lucky. We are in a civilized desert!

I'm worried he is not like other kids. I want to show him to a psychiatrist.

How did I come to drop my purse here? My husband was carrying it and he fell into it!

Amazing, Professor, what you just told me about the black holes up there millions and millions of miles away!

Don't shout! I cut it to create this abstract piece. I'll buy a dozen sarees for you when it is sold!

*He is really brilliant. He is listening to music on a
Walkman, talking on the cellular and also watching TV!*

When are you going to get permission from the Tree Lovers Association to cut this?

...and this is our Planning Division...

Before I type your report on this plant—isn't it the industrial plant the chairman wants the report on, Sir?

By the way, our old foreign collaborator retired handing over all his interests to him—his son!

I don't care how much it's going to cost! Don't go on repeating it! I want this economy measure implemented immediately!

I ruined his work of a lifetime! Instead of rushing towards the food when he rang the bell I ran in the opposite direction, deliberately!

He looks Japanese but he is a pucca Indian, really. I think we should employ him. It will do a great deal of good to the image of our company!

Look how he is using the bed! I had always thought he was the most scientific-minded among us!

All the computers are down with a virus attack. The Accounts Department is demanding extra pay to do the computers' work.

I started humbly as a hawker on this very pavement and built up my business steadily.

Poor chap is reduced to such a miserable state. The tax consultant he has hired holds only a fake degree!

The clarification has come, Sir, and it is confusing and vague. But it is better than the original government order which was misleading and muddled!

You always said I had a computer mind. Well this is a computer error. I can't account for Rs 50 lakh!

I am just carrying it for him! It seems the officers have formed a union.

Here he comes! Mark my word no business will be discussed. He will go on talking about cost of living, price of vegetables, milk, etc...

We had a quarrel! I said, 'Pack up your things and go!'. I didn't know everything belonged to her!

Peace of mind? Take a deep breath. Concentrate on your inner soul and meditate. You will attain peace of mind!

My wife will be very pleased to see you, Miss, and to know you are my new secretary!

This evening's gala function with the Chief Minister to give away the Industrial Safety Award is off, Sir! He has banged his fingers with the hammer while nailing! He is the awardee!

I told you when being appointed that I dealt firmly with situations and stood no nonsense. I am a product of a rather unconventional management school!

My foreign principals are coming for inspection and assessment. So I'll be away sight-seeing with them in Agra, Mahabalipuram, Ajanta, etc., for a fortnight!

*Don't be silly, Professor! All our research and studies have
shown this was extinct some two million years ago!*

OK, we will approach the World Bank. But first we must borrow from some other source to show we have the money. Otherwise it will refuse the loan!

Thanks Doctor, I am able to see far better now.

This year's budget is bad, anti-poor, pro-rich and will damage the economy! But personally, between you and me, it is pro-poor, will lead to growth, it is progressive and good.

No one knows what this section 59(Q) amendment 4-3CSQ stands for! But it very clearly says the violation of it is liable to fine and imprisonment up to five years!

Is this the breakthrough in karate you were so keen on demonstrating to me?

*No I can't employ your brother; that would be nepotism!
But I will order my secretary to give him a suitable job in
our organization.*

We should buy it. Rs 2 lakh is nothing considering he studied art in France for six years and has won many awards.

*That's what I call real salesmanship! The fellow just
walked in and sold me this hideous ash-tray much against
my determined consumer resistance! I want to offer him
our sales directorship!*

The Head Office says it has decided to move in here, Sir.
They find it cheaper than your frequent air-dashes to
Head Office and other expenses thereof.

I always felt these modern apartments were just not good for rock sessions!

He is an absolute liar! He goes about saying he is a close relative of Mickey Mouse!

The nice thing about this research lab is that the scientists here are all the time out attending seminars, leaving you completely undisturbed!

So sorry, the back-seat driver is responsible for it!

Is that the cigarette-lighter you told me you made your-self?

Eureka! I've discovered it—a way to emigrate!

Yes, I'll be rather busy this year; a seminar to attend on cold in Manila, another one in Hawaii on cough, yet another on headache in Rio...

Wipe off that I-told-you-so look!

Remember the test-tube baby? We had to keep on increasing the size of the test-tube—he refuses to step out.

This rare Himalayan herb will cure your headache. If it doesn't I'll give you a pill prepared by a famous multinational drug house.

I understand that air pollution from a nearby fertilizer plant did it!

OK, OK so you have made a plane which takes off vertically—now what have you done about its forward movement?

What a waste of time! When you kept saying 'Can't read, can't read', I didn't realise you didn't go to school!

Ah, that's what I like about indigenously manufactured units. They give sound advice!

Fertilizer is a very good thing. But a whole fertilizer factory next to them is no good for the plants.

*He would have gone into politics if he had been human—
the moment he learnt to talk he demanded mikes.*

Ah, I have traced the mistake, Professor. Instead of '1 + 2 = 3' you have written 4!

*We have chosen the wrong season for our adventure,
Sir!—the migratory birds are going to prove to be our
undoing.*

All that I asked the rascal was if he had a proper license for possessing the revolver!

*Don't let it go, Professor! You have caught a rare species
of butterfly with extraordinary strength!*

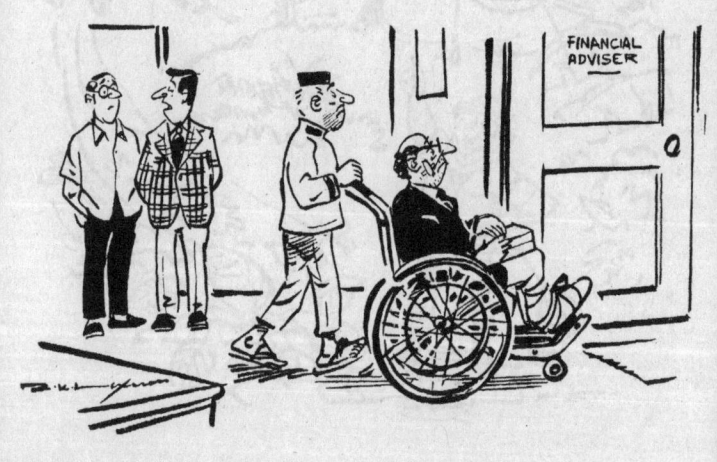

He tried to come to the office by bicycle to save petrol.

*Before going to attend another one of your seminars do
something about these work-kits, plastic bags, folders,
ball pens, pads that you bring back from the meetings!*

I am so sorry, Sir. The penalty is going to be pretty heavy. The small print in the contract you have signed does that...

In view of the miserable performance this year I have decided to sack all my 'yes men' and appoint new ones....!

Ah, I see the Russians seem to have already been there scooping the soil for tests.

Your invention, the cigarette lighter of the future is OK—but where will they get the fuel for it at that time?

Ah, here is our smart new engineer from the chemical plant to see us! Don't look so worried, young fellow: what's the problem?

We checked again, Sir. The finances are really not so bad.
There is a ledge on the first floor. You may, if you want
jump off quite safely from there!

*I asked you to get an enlarged picture of the isolated virus
and not the real one enlarged!*

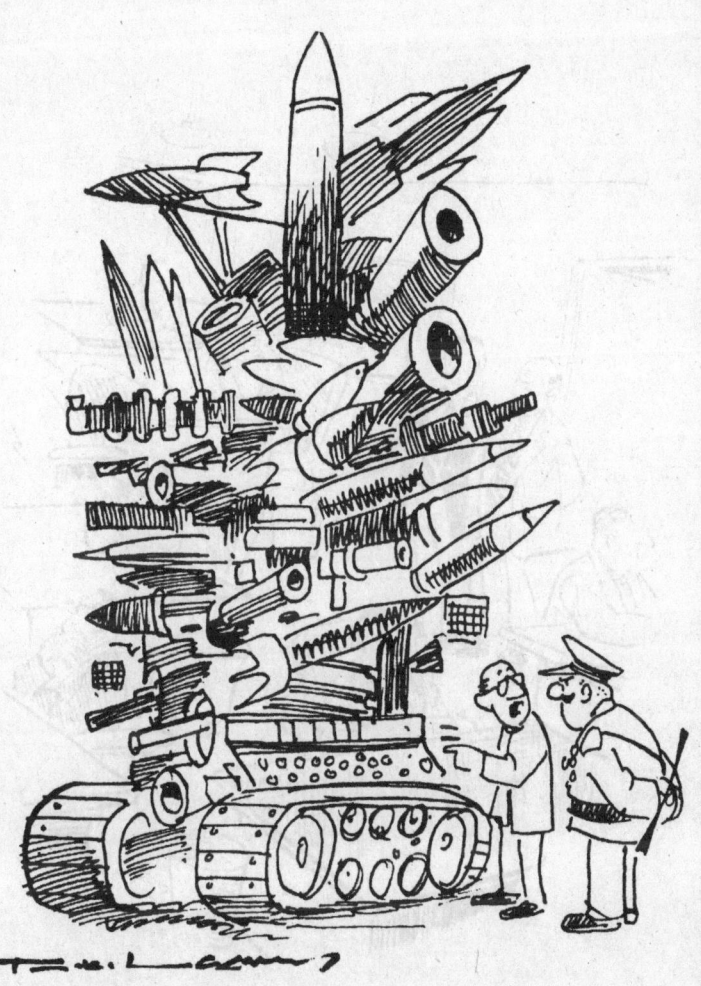

And finally, Field Marshal, if you press this button a pre-recorded statement of our peaceful intentions will be announced.

In this department we do not do any work; we do not have any statistics, data or information.

Just drop it into that tray, pick it up again and take it away. I have simplified the entire procedure!

I warn you! He will grow up to be a spoilt brat! You are letting him get away with the most unreasonable demands.

Help! Help! Yet another type of bug has attacked our computer!

There is definitely a snag in this garbage recycling plant—the end product is the same as the input.

*The staff gets on very well with me; strikes, go-slows,
demonstrations, etc. are unknown in this office.*

99

*He is from the International Pollution Control Authority.
He came to check the condition of our factory.*

I've got it! I have at last taught the antibodies karate!

*Here is the written explanation you wanted for my coming
late yesterday, Sir!*

As a humanitarian, I have combined in this the qualities of preserving people as well as their property.

Yes, I am reading a paper at the conference. The subject is 'Broader Application of the Concept of Delegation of Work and Duty'.

Let him go—no use holding down anyone who is unwilling to work here and wants to emigrate!

Before you sign the contract, young man I advise you to watch out for the clause, '...I am prepared to accept posting anywhere...' I overlooked that!

Tell that Sales Manager that not only should he improve sales but the whole sales pattern!

No Sir, I am not wasting time chatting with all sorts of people. That's my brother and his friend. Those two standing there are my brother-in-law and his nephew!

Yes Sir, the clarification sounds a bit confusing and vague but it is better than the original order which is misleading and incorrect.

*In the place I worked the Chief had made it so hot for me
I don't feel hot in here at all!*

*Yes, I warned him that if he continued to show indiffer-ence to work he wouldn't get a promotion. But he replied.
'That's OK I have plenty of job satisfaction'.*

My name, my qualifications, my designation all happen to be rather long!

I must say nepotism has great advantages sometimes. I just sacked my nephew without fear that the union will demand his reinstatement.

By the way, you should in no way think this new assignment is a reflection on your capability!

Still chatting, chatting! These youngsters are so careless—
they have no idea how expensive the use of the cellular is!

It's pre-dented, modelled on the cars already in use in the city, Sir!

*You should have briefed your client properly. He is
pleading 'not guilty' in his work-clothes!*

Of course, I am not going to retrench a single member of my staff. I ordered this all-purpose computer to help me in my official work, gentlemen. Any objections?

If you are looking for the pedestrian subway it's over there!

.....and the Complaints Department started for our employees' benefit has done well too; from 1,272 complaints in 1975 it went up to 2,763 in 1976...

We have to look for a telephone operator, a steno-typist, a filing clerk and a receptionist. I hear he has got a job in the Gulf.

And one more thing; don't call me 'Uncle' while we are in the office!

All preparations are ready except the subject. Can't think of one that has not been discussed before!

Good news for you! All this will not be yours one day, my son!

The next candidate please.

In appreciation of the excellent work you have been doing, the Chairman and the Board of Directors have decided to pay your salary of Rs 487 by cheque from now on!

My God! I came prepared thinking the subject was 'The Individual and Social Responsibilities'!

*Whatever you do you are criticized in this organization;
now they are complaining that I have spent too much in
reconstructing this factory!*

Yes, he just went up to the mike and returned, because that is all the time allotted to each speaker!

This was what I was afraid of; young executives returning with a strong rural bias after serving in our branches in those areas!

I was under the impression he had three sons!

No, he is not sacked—compulsory retirement!

That's a further step in evolution, my boy!—Look he is using a cellular phone.

*He just returned from Delhi today. But he went back
again and will be returning and going back early morning
tomorrow and…*

Of course, they all turn up punctually at 9.30 a.m. sharp as per your orders, Sir. But they go out again for an hour or so on personal work.

I still think you are making these oral tests pretty tough. Can't we just drop the candidate from selection if he gives wrong answers?

Oh, the talk is on real urban rats, is it?

The municipal water supply became so bad I thought of an easier way.

I have been kicked upstairs!

My God! This was rather a prolonged one... ...ich and
yet we did not talk a word of business! Shall we order
dinner and try?

Till now it was believed that you couldn't fool all the people all the time. I am happy to announce we have now achieved a breakthrough in that!

Just leave it like that. The cable is broken and I prefer this to the programmes they show.

You should not worry about failing in business. Take me for instance: I started a business taking a large loan and failed miserably once.

*All right, one more chance. I will pay another surprise
visit at the same time tomorrow. If I catch you two
chatting away again, I will take severe steps against you!*

It is true, then, what we heard about our new chairman; that he does not do anything without consulting his astrologer!

My son works there. He keeps sending up those anti-pollution messages all the time.

Son, I have decided to retire. Now you must take over my work in hiking the price of crude oil.

Smile, Your Honour!

*This obsession seizes you frequently—that you want to
enter politics and become the PM, right? That's normal.
Anything else?*

A close haircut and clean shave? Why, are you giving up being an artist, Sir?

Get lost boy! I don't want your chocolates, chewing gum, biscuits, peppermints. Can't you see I'm busy?

You are suffering from starvation. Don't use your solar cooker during monsoon—use the ordinary cooker.

The cash is with her, silly boy! You will know when you get married!

I'm glad you like it here—they give a lot of funds, equipment and leave you alone to do what you like!

...they can fix anything these days, kidney, heart, bone, eyes, hair—actually I myself am 96% transplant!

*Can't you find some other place to sell your delicious
preparation, my dear man?*

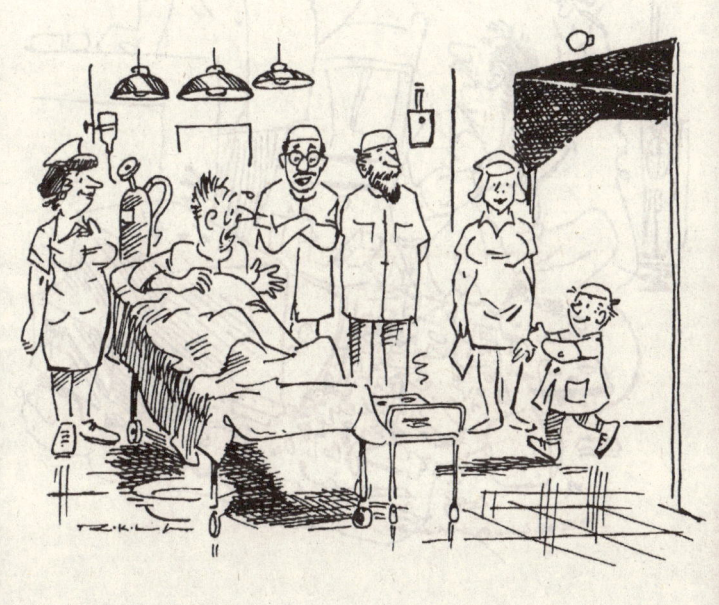

Didn't you know he is a child prodigy?

Nothing wrong with the TV, Sir. It's the plug which is defective.

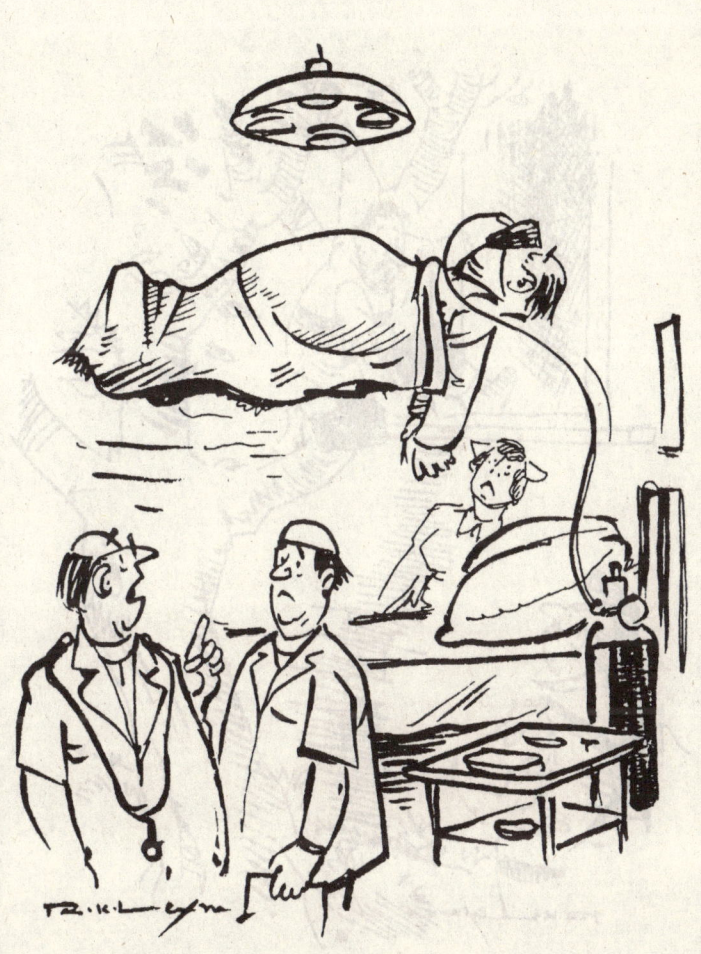

Look, young man, I clearly asked you to put him on oxygen and not hydrogen!

Don't get me wrong. My doctor has asked me not to climb steps!

What kind of salesman are you? You are selling the ball pen and giving away the TV free!

*Of course, the capitation fee for our medical course
includes charges for passport, visa, emigration facilities…*

Why are you saying 'Ah! Great! Wonderful!'? I'm yet to paint on it!

I knew the moment the government took over this would happen—we are asked to invent synthetic red tape at once.

*Look, that's your home! Remember that gun which melts
everything which we read about in the horror comic
book? Well, I've really made it!*

Clearly it's the influence of the movies.

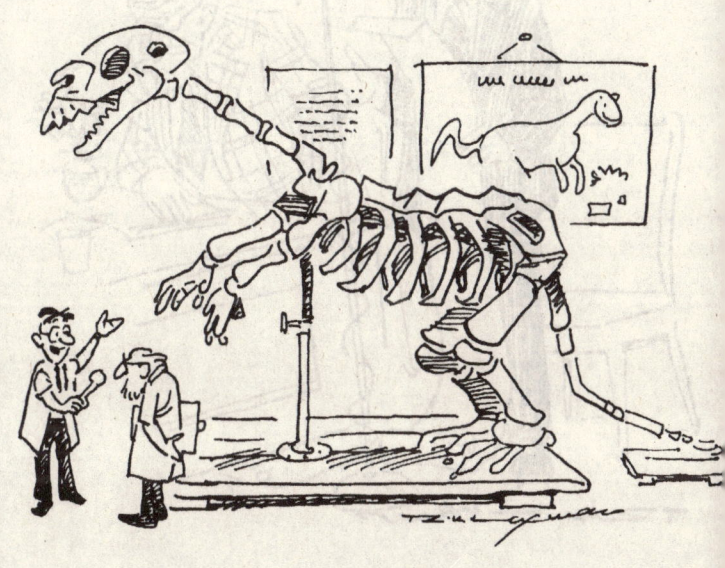

This piece doesn't fit in anywhere, Doctor So it isn't Dynopaplodiscerus as we thought but Dymonotoycorous.

Now, the Professor will give a short talk on scientific temper in the context of cooperative movements in developing countries in relation to international implications and technology of coordination…

I told you not to dabble in harnessing solar energy and to leave all that to the scientists.

A message from your son, Sir. He wants you in San Franscisco to manage his Transcendental Meditation Centre.

This is actually the research lab. But we have such a load of administrative work to do we can't conduct any experiments.

Are you crazy, Doctor? I am lying down and relaxing!

Must you bother me with these office matters when I'm so busy? Don't you know I am the President of Junior Chamber, Director of Executives Club, Secretary to the International Good League...

Look Miss, don't refer to the staff members as my brother-in-law, cousin, nephew, son-in-law etc. Address them as Sales Manager, PRO, Personnel Director, etc.

174

They brought a whole of lot of files and papers and got down to work. They just ordered two teas—supposed to be a business lunch!

*We all knew he had a nasty temper, Sir, when we took
him. But he is an asset to the company.—There has been
an all-round improvement since his appointment!*

There is something strange about that department, Sir. We retrenched 90% of the staff and yet it is functioning as smoothly as before!

Yes, I have rationalized my trade a bit. These days my clients are all businessmen and industrial magnates, you see!

He is a very nervous person. He always prays before signing any deal!

We are OK, gentlemen, we have made no application for takeover as a sick unit. It must be the industrial unit next door, which is really in a bad shape!

...even such small items like shaving blades, for instance, are manufactured without any concern for quality...

Good news, Professor, you've won an international award for your achievement! But you have to share it with him!

It saves a lot of bother. If you programme it, it goes about on its own taking pictures of tourist spots and historical interests, and returns.

Here is something which will save you from all this
drudgery—this computer will cut your work down by half.
But of course, your salary will also be cut in half accord-
ingly!

You want a younger man for the post, Sir? I was young when I was selected, but I got the appointment order only now. Perhaps it was due to procedural delay!

'Owing to unavoidable circumstances he could not come. However, he sent a warm message from Siberia wishing us success.'

Our export business was so good we even exported our entire factory!

He loves to have pictures of his wife and children on his table.

Still can't get it? Then call our agent in London to call my wife here to inform her I won't be coming for lunch. International calls are easier to get than local ones.

There has been considerable delay in the construction of the building. But his astrologer told him today was the most auspicious day to occupy his room.

Don't say you again forgot to administer the painkiller!

Every day after office he comes here and stands like that.
I am told the income by this is not taxable.

I was young and inexperienced and did not read the clause in small print in my contract properly and I am paying for it!

Hullo, Mumbai Stock Exchange?